Meet the family
my
Grandparents

by Mary Auld

W
FRANKLIN WATTS
LONDON•SYDNEY

This is Patrick with his dad's parents — Granny Frances and Grandpa Bill. They are two of Patrick's four grandparents.

This is James with his mum's dad. He calls him Grandad.

Sien and An were very sad when their grandpa died. They like to remember him by looking at photos of him with their parents.

Rosie's grandmother looks after her when her mum is at work.

Ed's grandparents live with him and the rest of the family.

Ali's grandpa is a doctor.

Claire's grandma
works in a shop.

Pete's grandpa is retired. Now he spends lots of time with Pete. They make all sorts of things together.

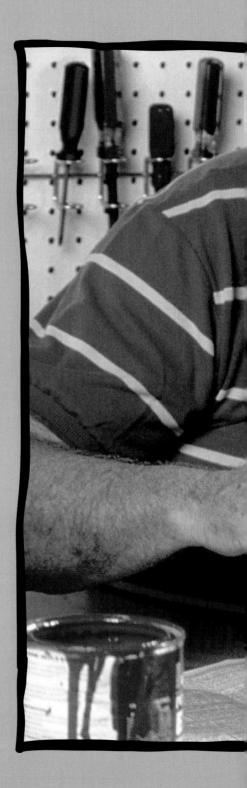

Kirstie likes staying the
night at her grandparents.

Mick's grandad takes him swimming.

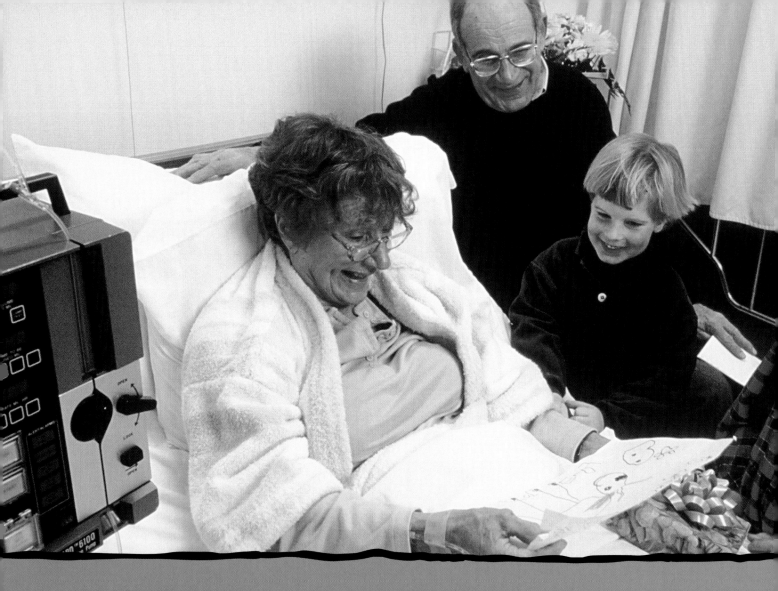

Ben's grandma isn't well.
Ben goes with his grandpa
to visit her in hospital.

Hannah's grandparents live a long way away — in another country. She often talks to them on the phone.

This is Saffron with her mum, her granny and her mum's granny – Saffron's great-granny.

What are your grandparents like?

Family words

Here are some words people use when talking about their grandparents or family.

Names for grandparents:
Gran, Granny, Grandma, Grandmother;
Grandad, Grandpa, Grandfather.

Names for parents:
Father, Daddy, Dad, Pa;
Mother, Mummy, Mum, Ma.

Names of other relatives:
Sister, Brother; Daughter, Son;
Uncle; Aunt, Auntie; Nephew; Niece.

If we put the word 'great' in front of a relative's name it means that they are separated from us by an extra generation of family. Look at the family tree on page 24; each level on it is a generation.

A family tree

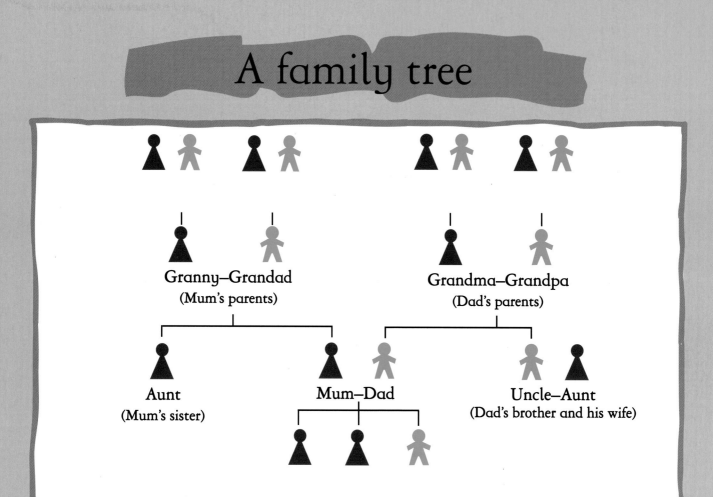

Granny–Grandad
(Mum's parents)

Grandma–Grandpa
(Dad's parents)

Aunt
(Mum's sister)

Mum–Dad

Uncle–Aunt
(Dad's brother and his wife)

You can show how you are related to all your family on a plan like this one. It is called a family tree. Every family tree is different. Try drawing your own.

This edition published in 2008 by Franklin Watts, 338 Euston Road, London NW1 3BH

Franklin Watts Australia
Level 17/207 Kent Street, Sydney NSW 2000
Copyright © Franklin Watts 2003

Series editor: Rachel Cooke
Art director: Jonathan Hair
Design: Andrew Crowson
A CIP catalogue record for this book is available from the British Library.

ISBN 978 0 7496 8108 1

Acknowledgements:
Bruce Berman/Corbis: front cover centre below. www.johnbirdsall.co.uk: front cover top, 12, 17. Jon Feingersh/Corbis: 9. Carlos Goldin/Corbis: front cover main, 22. Sally Greenhill/Sally & Richard Greenhill PL: 5, 10-11. Tom & Dee Ann McCarthy/Corbis: 6, 19b. Brian Mitchell/Photofusion: 16. Jose Luis Pelaez/Corbis: front cover bottom, 19cl. Karen Robinson/Photofusion: 13. George Shelley/Corbis: front cover centre above. Ariel Skelley/Corbis: front cover centre, 20. Liz Somerville/Photofusion: 2. Tom Stewart/Corbis: 18. David Woods/Corbis: 1, 14-15.

Franklin Watts is a division of Hachette Children's Books, an Hachette Livre UK company.
www.hachettelivre.co.uk

Printed in Hong Kong/China

Please note that some of the pictures in this book have been posed by models.